W9-CQF-307

POM-POM MANIA

POM-POM MANIA

Create **8** pom-pom pals for you and your friends

PaRRagon

Bath • New York • Cologne • Melbourne • Delhi
Hong Kong • Shenzhen • Singapore • Amsterdam

LIFE IS BETTER WITH A POM-POM

This edition published by Parragon Books Ltd in 2014
and distributed by

Parragon Inc.
440 Park Avenue South, 13th Floor
New York, NY 10016
www.parragon.com

Copyright © Parragon Books Ltd 2014

Crafts and sketches by Kate Woods
Designed by Mark Dyment
Illustrations by Holly Maguire
Photography by Henry Sparrow
Project managed by Frances Prior-Reeves

All rights reserved. No part of this publication may be reproduced,
stored in a retrieval system, or transmitted, in any form or by any
means, electronic, mechanical, photocopying, recording, or
otherwise, without the prior permission of the copyright holder.

ISBN 978-1-4723-5238-5

Printed in China

This book is sold subject to the condition that all designs and instructions contained in it are copyrighted and not for
commercial reproduction without the permission of the publisher, Parragon Books Ltd.

To the fullest extent permitted by law, the author and the publisher: (i) cannot and do not accept any legal duty of care or
responsibility in relation to the accuracy or appropriateness of the contents of this book; and (ii) disclaim any liability, loss,
damage, or risk that may be claimed or incurred as a consequence—directly or indirectly—of the use and/or attempted use
of any of the contents of this book.

The craft activities in this book may present small parts so it is recommended that the finished items are not given to
children under 3 years.

INTRODUCTION

How this book works

This book contains eight adorable pom-pom characters for you to make. You can find pom-poms almost anywhere; on top of beanies, on slippers, or at the ends of scarves, but they come into their own as pom-pom animals. If you're looking for something cute and simple to get you started, begin with the Hedgehog on page 12.

This book has an array of cute characters you'll love making, and you can even create a whole tribe of them. Each project contains step-by-step instructions to follow, with helpful illustrations on the final page of the project. If an instruction has an illustration for it, it is shown by this symbol ✸ and the corresponding number will be seen next to the illustration.

The instructions for each project include a list of materials. It's worth noting that for all eight projects you will always need some basic craft supplies: thick cardboard, pencil, ruler, scissors, needle, and craft glue. Since these items are needed for every project we've not included them in the lists of materials.

Some of the projects require specific additional materials, which are available to buy in all good craft stores or online. Before embarking on any of the projects, take a moment to look through the list of materials for each to ensure you have everything you need. Templates are provided for all eight projects and these are included in the back of the book, starting on page 44. Also see the tips on page 11. Crafting is lots of fun, but you do need to read through each project carefully before you start, to avoid the frustration of discovering you don't have everything you need!

Remember to keep any spare wool and always say yes to anyone who is throwing out any bundles of wool. You can also use scraps of felt and spare ribbon left over from other craft projects, as only a small amount is required. All the projects in this book are super easy and can be made in an afternoon. They make great gifts, or you may just want to make one for yourself.

You won't need any special equipment to make pom-poms. You can use tools and materials that you probably already have. Here is a basic list to get you started.

Large scissors

You will need these for cutting the wool and creating a rough pom-pom.

Embroidery scissors

Fine, sharp scissors are useful for trimming the pom-pom into a precise and neat shape.

Large needle

A needle with an eye big enough to thread wool is necessary to secure two pom-poms together.

Embroidery floss and needle

Black embroidery floss is useful to sew details onto the faces of the pom-pom animals, using a basic straight stitch, or you can use any color of your choice.

Beads and buttons

Small round black beads or buttons would work as eyes for most of the projects, although you can also buy beads designed to look like eyes (such as for the Teddy on page 24). If you don't have access to any of these, eyes can be quickly and easily cut from felt.

Ribbon

Ribbon is used in a few of the projects, but you will only need a small amount. You can use up small scraps left over from other craft projects.

Felt

This is an easy material to use as it doesn't fray, is easy to cut, and is easy to glue. It is readily available at an affordable price from most craft stores or online.

Glue

Craft glue, available from most good craft stores, is necessary to glue the felt pieces to the pom-pom to create eyes, noses, beaks, ears, tails, etc. You can also dab glue between two pom-poms before binding them together, to make them extra secure. Superglue can also be used to secure mini pom-poms to larger pom-poms.

types of yarn

Wool is a universal term that covers many types of yarn. Most "wool" yarns are probably a mix of acrylic and wool, making them less prone to shrinkage when washed, but you can find some wool that is a hundred percent pure new wool. What matters when making pom-poms is the look and feel of the wool after it's been trimmed.

Wool

Thick wool creates a larger, rougher pom-pom, and thin wool is easier to trim to a neater, smaller shape. Very thick wool can be used to make a very textured pom-pom, such as for the Owl project on page 36, and multicolored thick wool is great for creating the look of feathers. Thin wool is better for small, tightly packed pom-poms, such as for the tail of the Rabbit on page 20.

Mohair

This is a silklike yarn made from the hair of a goat. It is great for making downy pom-poms that are extra fluffy.

Alpaca

This unusual yarn looks similar to wool but is even softer. It comes from animals that look something like llamas. Use it to make supersoft pom-poms.

Silk—wool blend

A silk—wool blend makes dense, shiny pom-poms. Try it as a replacement for thin wool.

It is important to note that all weights mentioned in the projects are approximate and it depends on how tightly you wrap the wool and how thick the wool is. If in doubt, it is better to use too much and trim it down than to use too little.

How to make a basic pom-pom

Materials:

Thick cardboard

Wool (approx 1 ¼ oz/35 g; binding: approx 12 in/30 cm)

Scissors

Here's how to make a basic pom-pom. This is the size used most often throughout the book.

1. Cut a thick piece of cardboard, roughly 4½ in x 2¾ in/12 cm x 7 cm.

2. Wrap the wool around the cardboard. Wrap it around with consistent and gentle tension, making sure it is not too tight, and wrap it evenly along the length of the cardboard. Tuck the last bit of wool into the wool wrap.

3. Gently slide the bundle of wool off the cardboard, making sure you keep hold of it so that it doesn't unravel. Using a piece of wool 12 in/30 cm long, wrap the wool around the bundle horizontally, making sure it is tight. It will squeeze the wrapped wool together in the middle.

4. Slide the blade of your scissors into the loops of the bundle and gradually work your way around, until you have a rough pom-pom.

5. Trim the pom-pom to the required shape and size.

Trimming the pom-pom

Wrapping the yarn around the cardboard, before binding and cutting the edges to make the rough pom-pom, is easy. The "art" is in the trimming of the pom-pom to get the shape you want. If you are a beginner worried about your trimming skills, wrap the wool much more thickly around the cardboard to create a denser pom-pom or use a wider cardboard template to create a longer stranded pom-pom and then trim it down. Having more wool doesn't matter; it just packs tighter together for a rougher look. Make it as big as you want and then slowly trim it down until you get more confident.

basic techniques

Making pom-poms of different sizes

You can make a basic pom-pom of any size, depending on the size of the cardboard you wrap the wool around and the amount of wool you use. Make a denser pom-pom by wrapping more wool around the cardboard and a longer or shorter stranded pom-pom by reducing or enlarging the size of the cardboard. You can even use a table fork to make mini pom-poms (see below).

How to make a mini pom-pom

Materials

Fork, Wool (approx 1/8 oz/5 g; binding: 2 in/5 cm), Scissors

1. Using a fork, wrap the wool around the prongs evenly along its length. Slide the bundle of wool off the fork, making sure you keep hold of it so it doesn't unravel.

2. Then using another length of wool, tie a tight knot around the bundle of wool. It will squeeze the wrapped wool together in the middle.

3. Slide the blade of your scissors into the loops of the bundle and gradually work your way around, until you have a rough pom-pom, in a smaller size.

4. Trim the mini pom-pom to the required shape and size.

How to make a two-color pom-pom

Materials

Thick cardboard, Ruler, Pencil, Scissors

Two shades of Wool (approx 1 1/4 oz/each 35 g; binding: 12 in/30 cm)

1. Cut a piece of thick cardboard, roughly 4½ in x 2¾ in/12 cm x 7 cm. Measure 2½ in/6 cm along the longer side and draw a vertical line down the cardboard to mark the halfway point.

2. Using the line as a guide, wrap one of the shades of wool around half of the cardboard. Wrap it around with consistent and gentle tension, making sure it is not too tight, and wrap it evenly along the length of the cardboard. The wool shouldn't be fatter in the middle. Tuck the last bit of wool into the wool wrap.

3. Wrap the other shade of wool around the other half of the cardboard in the same way. Tuck the last bit of wool into the wool wrap.

4. Gently slide the bundle of wool off the cardboard, making sure you keep hold of it so that it doesn't unravel. Using a piece of wool 12 in/30 cm long, wrap the wool around the bundle horizontally, making sure it is tight. It will squeeze the wrapped wool together in the middle.

5. Slide the blade of your scissors into the loops of the bundle and gradually work your way around, until you have a rough pom-pom.

6. Trim the pom-pom to the required shape and size.

Tips for transferring templates to felt

You will need to use the templates in this book to cut out the shapes of the ears, feet, and other parts of your pom-pom animals.

There are several ways of using a template and transferring a design to fabric. This is the easiest and least expensive way:

1. Photocopy the relevant templates for the chosen project. You can increase or reduce the size on a photocopier if you are making smaller or larger pom-poms than instructed.

2. Pin the photocopy of the template on top of the felt, making sure to secure it in place with enough pins so that it won't move when you start cutting.

3. Cut out the shapes through the two layers, using the lines of the photocopy as a guide.

TIPS! Remember not to wrap the wool around the cardboard too tightly, or you will never manage to get it off.

When in doubt keep wrapping the wool around the cardboard; the more wool you use the denser the pom-pom.

Don't worry when you trim your pom-pom: start off slowly and stop from time to time to check the shape.

You can use any yarn to make a pom-pom: hairy, soft, fat, or thin. Once you have perfected your craft, start being more adventurous and use strips of fabric, paper, and even tissue paper.

Get everyone involved. Kids and adults will love making them!

HEDGEHOG

This adorable hedgehog won't give you any unwanted prickly encounters — her soft, shaggy spikes make her look completely huggable. This pom-pom hedgehog is made using two different shades of wool in one pom-pom and then cut to give an individual personality. Why not make a friend to keep her company?

. . . .

materials you'll need

Brown Wool
(head: approx ⅛ oz/5 g;
body: approx ⅛ oz/5 g)

Cream wool
(head: approx ⅛ oz/5 g;
body: approx ⅛ oz/5 g;
binding for head and body:
approx 32 in/80 cm long)

Templates from page 44

Brown felt

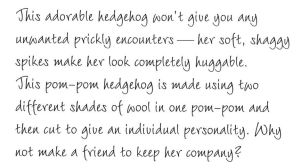

1. Cut a piece of thick cardboard, roughly 4½ in x 2¾ in/12 cm x 7 cm. Measure 2½ in/ 6 cm along the longer side and draw a vertical line down the cardboard to mark the halfway point.

2. Using the line as a guide, wrap the brown wool around half of the cardboard. Wrap it around with consistent and gentle tension and make sure to wrap it evenly across the length of the card. The wool shouldn't be fatter in the middle. Tuck the last bit of wool into the wool wrap.

   TIP! Don't wrap the wool too tightly around the cardboard; otherwise you will have trouble getting the bound wool off later.

3. Wrap the cream wool around the other half of the cardboard in the same way as the brown wool. Tuck the last bit of wool into the wool wrap.

MAKE
ME
TODAY

13

4. Gently slide the bundle of wool off the cardboard, making sure you keep hold of it so that it doesn't unravel. Using a piece of cream wool 12 in/30 cm long, wrap the wool around the bundle horizontally, making sure it is tight. It will squeeze the wrapped wool together in the middle. ✹

5. Slide the blade of your scissors into the loops of the bundle and gradually work your way around, until you have a rough pom-pom.

6. Repeat steps 1 to 5 to create a second identical pom-pom. One will become the head and one will become the body of your Hedgehog.

7. Shape one of the pom-poms to form the Hedgehog's head. The cream part needs to be smaller than the brown part. Leave the brown wool looking shaggy, as this is the Hedgehog's spines. ✹

8. Shape the second pom-pom to form the body.

9. Using a large needle threaded with cream wool approx 8 in/20 cm long, thread the needle through the bottom of the body and up through the head. Loop the wool back through the top of the head and through the body, then tie in a knot at the bottom to hold them together. You can dab glue between the head and body before sewing to make it extra secure. ✹

10. Photocopy the templates for the Hedgehog from page 44. Use the template as a guide to cut out the Hedgehog's ears, feet, eyes, paws, and nose from brown felt.

11. Apply glue to the straight edges of the ears and wedge them into the side of the pom-pom head at the margin between the cream and brown wool. Repeat for the paws so that they are positioned at the top of the pom-pom body. ✹

12. Glue the Hedgehog's eyes and nose in place to create the face.

13. Apply glue to the feet and position underneath the body. Your Hedgehog should look like the photo on page 13.

TIP! Flatten the base of the pom-pom body so that the Hedgehog stands upright before you glue the feet in place.

4.

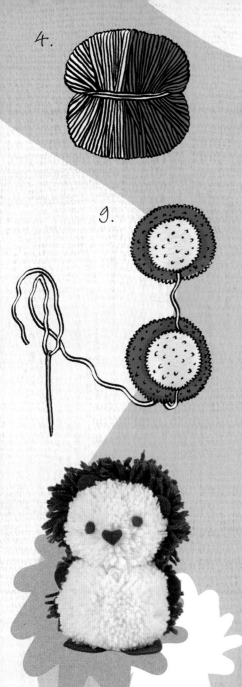

7.

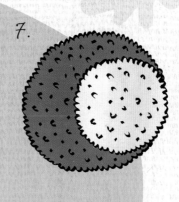

9.

11.

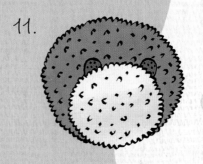

VARIATION

Try using different accessories for different hedgehogs to create different characters. For example, tie a ribbon into a bow and glue to the top of the Hedgehog's head. You could use a two-tone wool for the Hedgehog's spines, in place of the brown, to give her more texture.

15

KING
POM

LION

There's nothing to fear from this cuddly, pom-pom lion as he's so easy to make. Made from two different shades of wool, felt, and a few beads, he'll be ready to growl in no time. Don't stop there, however. You could make a whole pride of lions in various shades of wool and different sizes.

materials you'll need

Thick orange wool
(head: approx 1¼ oz/35 g
body: approx 1¼ oz/35 g)

Yellow wool
(head: approx 1¼ oz/35 g
body: approx 1¼ oz/35 g
binding for head and body:
approx 32 in/80 cm long)

Templates from page 44

Orange felt

White felt

One plastic nose

Two plastic eyes

1. Cut a piece of thick cardboard, roughly 4½ in x 2¾ in/12 cm x 7 cm. Measure 2¼ in/6 cm along the longer side and draw a vertical line down the cardboard to mark the halfway point.

2. Using the line as a guide, wrap the orange wool around half of the cardboard. Wrap it around with consistent and gentle tension and make sure to wrap it evenly across the length of the cardboard. The wool shouldn't be fatter in the middle. Tuck the last bit of wool into the wool wrap.

TIP! Don't wrap the wool too tightly around the cardboard, otherwise you will have trouble getting the bound wool off later.

3. Wrap the yellow wool around the other half of the cardboard in the same way as the orange wool. Tuck the last bit of wool into the wool wrap. ✸

4. Gently slide the bundle of wool off the cardboard, making sure you keep hold of it so that it doesn't unravel. Using a piece of yellow wool 12 in/30 cm long, wrap the wool around the bundle horizontally, making sure it is tight. It will squeeze the wrapped wool together in the middle.

5. Slide the blade of your scissors into the loops of the bundle and gradually work your way around, until you have a rough pom-pom.

6. Repeat steps 1 to 5 to create a second identical pom-pom. One will become the head and one will become the body of your Lion.

7. Shape one of the pom-poms to form the Lion's head. The yellow part needs to be smaller than the orange part. Leave the orange wool looking shaggy, as this is the Lion's mane. ✺

8. Shape the second pom-pom to form the body. Make sure you leave the top part of the yellow wool a little shaggy to look like the Lion's neck.

9. Using a large needle threaded with yellow wool approx 8 in/20 cm long, thread the needle through the bottom of the body and up through the head. Loop the wool back through the top of the head and through the body, then tie

in a knot at the bottom to hold them together. You can dab glue between the head and body before sewing to make it extra secure.

10. Photocopy the templates for the Lion from page 44. Use the template as a guide to cut out the Lion's ears, feet, and tail from orange felt.

11. Apply glue to the straight edge of the Lion's tail and wedge it into the back of the body. ✺

12. Using the template from page 44 as a guide, cut out the Lion's mouth from white felt. Cut a small hole in the top of the felt, insert the nose bead and glue in place, in the center of the Lion's head. ✺

TIP! You can reduce or increase the size of the templates on a photocopier, if you want to make the Lion in different sizes.

13. Apply glue to the straight edges of the ears and wedge them into the sides of the pom-pom head. Apply glue to the feet and position underneath the body. Glue the beads for the eyes onto the head of the Lion. Leave to dry. Your Lion should look like the photo on page 16.

3.

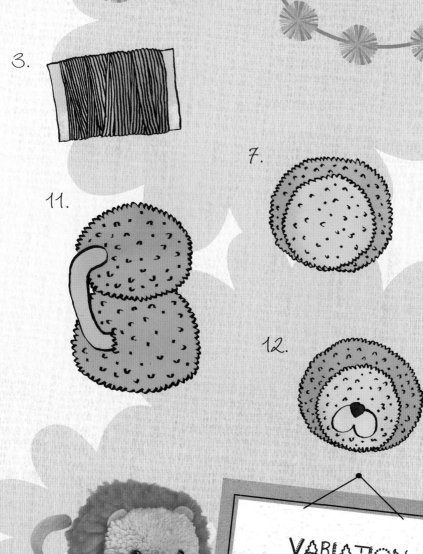

7.

11.

12.

VARIATION

Use a two-tone thick wool for the head in place of the orange wool, to make the Lion's mane really distinctive and bushy.

MINI POM TAIL

RABBIT

This fluffy bunny, made using two shades of wool and shapes cut from felt, is a perfect springtime partner for Bird on page 32. His cute little pom-pom tail is cleverly crafted using just a fork and some white wool. He can easily be adapted to make lots of bunnies in various shades.

. . . .

materials you'll need

White wool
(body: approx 1 1/4 oz/35 g;
tail: 1/8 oz/5 g;
binding for tail:
approx 2 in/5 cm)

Light brown wool
(body: approx 1 1/4 oz/35 g;
head: 1 oz/25 g;
binding for head and body:
approx 32 in/80 cm)

Fork

Templates from page 45

Light brown felt

Pink felt

White felt

Two plastic eyes

1. Cut a piece of thick cardboard, roughly 4½ in x 2¾ in 12 cm x 7 cm. Measure 2½ in/6 cm along the longer side and draw a vertical line down the cardboard to mark the halfway point.

2. Using the line as a guide, wrap the white wool around half of the cardboard. Wrap it around with consistent and gentle tension, making sure it is not too tight, and wrap it evenly across the length of the card. The wool shouldn't be fatter in the middle. Tuck the last bit of wool into the wool wrap.

TIP! To make bigger and denser pom-poms, make the cardboard wider and wrap more wool around it.

3. Wrap the brown wool around the other half of the cardboard in the same way as the white wool. Tuck the last bit of wool into the wool wrap.

4. Gently slide the bundle of wool off the cardboard, making sure you keep hold of it so that it doesn't unravel. Using a piece of light brown wool 12 in/30 cm long, wrap the wool around the bundle horizontally, making sure it is tight. It will squeeze the wrapped wool together in the middle.

5. Slide the blade of your scissors into the loops of the bundle and gradually work your way around, until you have a rough pom-pom. ✸

6. Repeat steps 1 to 5 for the Rabbit's head, but use only light brown wool, wrapping it around the card in the same way, to form a slightly smaller pom-pom.

7. To make the tail, wrap the white wool around the prongs of a fork, making sure it is not too tight and is wrapped evenly along the length of the fork. ✸
Slide the bundle of wool off the fork, making sure you keep hold of it so it doesn't unravel. Then, using another piece of white wool 2 in/5 cm long, tie a tight knot around the bundle of wool. It will squeeze the wrapped wool together in the middle.

8. Slide the blade of your scissors into the loops of the bundle and gradually work your way around, until you have another rough pom-pom, in a smaller size.

9. Trim the brown pom-pom to form a neat round shape for the Rabbit's head and the small white pom-pom to form a round shape for the Rabbit's tail. Trim the white and brown pom-pom, making the white part slightly smaller than the brown, to form the Rabbit's body. ✸

10. Using a large needle threaded with white wool 8 in/20 cm long, thread the needle through the bottom of the body and up through the head. Loop the wool back through the top of the head and through the body, then tie in a knot at the bottom to hold them together. You can dab glue between the head and body before sewing to make it more secure.

11. Glue the small white pom-pom to the back of the Rabbit's body to form the tail.

12. Photocopy the templates from page 45. Using the templates as a guide, cut out the Rabbit's outer ears, feet, and paws from the brown felt; the Rabbit's inner ears and nose from the pink felt; and the Rabbit's mouth and two teeth from the white felt. Glue the Rabbit's pink inner ears to the brown outer ears and leave to dry. Once dry, pinch the bottom edges of the ears together and stitch with brown wool to secure. ✸

13. Glue the Rabbit's pink nose onto the white mouth and glue two white teeth under the mouth. When dry, glue to the center of the Rabbit's head. ✸

14. Add glue to the pinched edges of the ears and wedge the ears into the top of the Rabbit's head. Add glue to the flat edges of the Rabbit's paws and wedge into the sides of the body. Glue and position the Rabbit's feet underneath the body.

15. Glue the Rabbit's eyes to the head and leave to dry. Your Rabbit should look like the photo on page 20.

5.

7.

9.

12.

VARIATION

Use different shades of wool to create more rabbits. You could make a completely white Rabbit using just white wool, instead of brown and white. Try white and pink felt for the ears, pale pink felt for the mouth, darker pink felt for the nose, and cream felt for the teeth.

13.

TEDDY

A dashing red scarf gives this lovable teddy plenty of style, topped off with his mini black top hat. All you will need to make are two larger gray pom-poms and four mini pom-poms; add some felt, a nose, and two eyes, and he comes to life as if by magic.

. . . .

1. Cut a piece of thick cardboard, roughly 4½ in x 2¾ in/ 12 cm x 7 cm.

2. Wrap the gray wool around the card with consistent and gentle tension, making sure it is not too tight, and wrap it evenly across the length of the card. The wool shouldn't be fatter in the middle. Tuck the last bit of wool into the wool wrap.

3. Gently slide the bundle of wool off the cardboard, making sure you keep hold of it so that it doesn't unravel. Using a piece of wool 12 in/30 cm long, wrap the wool around the bundle horizontally, making sure it is tight. It will squeeze the wrapped wool together in the middle.

4. Slide the blade of your scissors into the loops of the bundle and gradually work your way around, until you have a rough pom-pom.

5. Repeat steps 1 to 4 for the Teddy's head to create a slightly smaller pom-pom. ✱

materials you'll need

Thick gray wool
(body: approx 1¼ oz/35 g;
head: approx 1 oz/25 g;
ears and feet: ⅛ oz/5 g x 4;
binding for head and body:
40 in/100 cm)

Fork

Templates from page 45

White felt, Red felt, Black felt

Plastic nose, Two plastic eyes

Black embroidery floss

Thin cardboard

POSH POM

25

6. Using a fork, wrap the wool evenly around the prongs. Slide the bundle of wool off the fork, making sure you keep hold of it so it doesn't unravel. Then using another piece of wool 2 in/5 cm long, tie a tight knot around the bundle of wool. It will squeeze the wrapped wool together in the middle.

7. Slide the blade of your scissors into the loops of the bundle and gradually work your way around until you have a rough pom-pom, in a much smaller size than the head and body. Do this four times to create two ears and two feet. ✻

8. Trim the larger pom-poms to form a round shape for the Teddy's head and a larger round shape for the body. Trim the four small pom-poms to create four neat round shapes for the ears and feet.

9. Photocopy the templates on page 45. Using the templates as a guide, cut the Teddy's nose from white felt. Cut a small hole in the felt and insert the black plastic nose, then glue in place. Using a needle and black floss, stitch a vertical line underneath the black nose. Glue the felt to the Teddy's head. ✻

10. Using a large needle threaded with wool about 8 in/20 cm long, thread the needle through the bottom of the body and up through the head. Loop the wool back through the top of the head and through the body, then tie in a knot at the bottom, to hold them together. You can dab glue between the head and body to make it more secure, before sewing.

11. Glue two of the small pom-poms to the sides of the head to form the ears. Glue the remaining two small pom-poms at the front of the body to form the feet.

TIP! You can use superglue to secure the small pom-poms in place, if craft glue isn't strong enough.

12. Glue the plastic eyes above the nose on the head and leave to dry completely.

13. Using the templates on page 45, cut out the scarf from red felt. It needs to be 13 in/33 cm long and 1¼ in/3 cm wide. Cut slits to form a fringe at each end of the scarf. Tie it around the Teddy's neck, securing in place with glue. ✻

14. To make Teddy's hat, use the templates on page 45 as a guide and cut out three pieces of thin cardboard as follows: a rectangle 5½ in x 1½ in/14 cm x 4 cm for the hat side, a circle with a diameter of 1¼ in/3 cm for the hat top, and a circle with a diameter of 1¾ in/4.5 cm for the h brim. Cut out the same shapes from the black fe

15. Roll the long piece of cardboard and secure wit glue to form a tube with a diameter of 1¼ in/3 cm. Glue the long piece of black felt to the outside of the tube. Glue the larger circle of bla felt to the larger circle of cardboard and the sm circle of black felt to the small circle of cardboar

16. Once dry, glue the smaller circle to the top of th tube, then glue the larger circle to the bottom o the tube with the felt facing up. It should resemb a small top hat. Leave to dry, then glue the finish hat to the top of Teddy's head. Your Teddy shoul look like the photo on page 25. ✻

5.

7.

9.

13.

16.

VARIATION

Make six mini pom-poms instead of four and glue two to the sides of Teddy's body to form arms and two to the bottom to form legs. The remaining two are Teddy's ears. Replace the scarf with a ribbon tied in a bow around Teddy's neck and omit the hat.

WIRE WHISKERS

CAT

This lucky cat is so easy to make from just two pom-poms. Using craft wire and glue, you can give her lovely long whiskers. You could even make smaller versions and give her some kittens.

materials you'll need

White wool
(body: approx 1 1/4 oz/35 g)

Black wool
(body: approx 1 1/4 oz/35 g;
head: approx 1 oz/25 g;
binding for head and body:
approx 32 in/80 cm)

Templates from page 46

Black felt, White felt,
Pink Felt

Two plastic eyes

Black embroidery floss

Craft wire

1. Cut a piece of thick cardboard, roughly 4½ in x 2¾ in/12 cm x 7 cm. Measure 2½ in/6 cm along the longer side and draw a vertical line down the cardboard to mark the halfway point.

2. Using the line as a guide, wrap the white wool around half of the cardboard. Wrap it around with consistent and gentle tension, making sure it is not too tight, and wrap it evenly along the length of the card. The wool shouldn't be fatter in the middle. Tuck the last bit of wool into the wool wrap.

3. Wrap the black wool around the other half of the cardboard in the same way. Tuck the last bit of wool into the wool wrap.

TIP! Any two colors of wool could be used here to create different colored cats, or one multicolored wool to create a tabby.

4. Gently slide the bundle of wool off the cardboard, making sure you keep hold of it so that it doesn't unravel. Using a piece of black wool 12 in/30 cm long, wrap the wool around the bundle horizontally, making sure it is tight. It will squeeze the wrapped wool together in the middle.

5. Slide the blade of your scissors into the loops of the bundle and gradually work your way around, until you have a rough pom-pom.

6. Repeat steps 1 to 5 for the Cat's head, using black wool to create a slightly smaller pom-pom.

7. Trim the black pom-pom to form a neat round shape for the Cat's head. Trim the black and white pom-pom, making the white part slightly smaller than the black, to form the Cat's body. ✸

8. Using a large needle threaded with black wool 8 in/20 cm long, thread the needle through the bottom of the body and up through the head. Loop the wool back through the top of the head and through the body and tie in a knot at the bottom to hold them together. You can also dab glue between the head and the body to make it extra secure before sewing.

9. Photocopy the templates on page 46. Using the template as a guide, cut the Cat's outer ears from black felt and the inner ears from white felt. Glue the white felt to the black felt and leave to dry. ✸

10. Using the templates on page 46 as a guide, cut the shape of the Cat's mouth from white felt. Cut the Cat's nose from pink felt. Glue the nose onto the mouth and leave to dry. Using a needle and black floss, stitch a vertical line from the bottom of the nose to the lower edge of the white felt. ✸

11. Apply glue to the straight edge of each ear and wedge the ears into the sides of the pom-pom head. Glue the nose to the face and glue the plastic eyes above it.

12. Cut the craft wire into six 2½-in/6-cm lengths. Apply glue to the ends of the craft wire whiskers and wedge the whiskers behind the mouth/nose. Leave to dry. ✸

TIP! You can use superglue to secure the whiskers in place, if craft glue is not strong enough.

13. Using the template on page 46, cut out the tail from black felt and wedge into the back of the body pom-pom. Leave to dry. Your Cat should look like the photo on page 28. ✸

7.

9.

10.

12.

13.

VARIATION

Make kittens by reducing the size of the cardboard and the amount of wool used. Use smaller beads for the eyes and reduce the size of the templates to make ears and a tail of the right proportions.

BIRD

Bird has a unique personality of her own. Her shape is all about the trimming of the pom-poms. Create a fluffy tail by leaving the pom-pom for her body slightly longer and rougher on one side. You can also change the color to make a chick.

. . . .

1. Cut a piece of thick cardboard, roughly 4½ in x 2¾ in/12 cm x 7 cm.

2. Wrap the blue wool around the cardboard. Wrap it around with consistent and gentle tension, making sure it is not too tight, and wrap it evenly along the length of the cardboard. The wool shouldn't be fatter in the middle. Tuck the last bit of wool into the wool wrap.

3. Gently slide the bundle of wool off the cardboard, making sure you keep hold of it so that it doesn't unravel. Using a piece of wool 12 in/30 cm long, wrap the wool around the bundle horizontally, making sure it is tight. It will squeeze the wrapped wool together in the middle. ✳

materials you'll need

Blue wool
(body: approx 1 ¼ oz/35 g;
head: approx 1 oz/25 g;
binding for head and body:
32 in/80 cm)

Templates from page 46

Light green felt

Orange felt

Two plastic eyes

Teal ribbon

FLYING POM

33

4. Slide the blade of your scissors into the loops of the bundle and gradually work your way around, until you have a rough pom-pom.

5. Repeat steps 1 to 4 for the Bird's head, using less wool to create a slightly smaller pom-pom.

6. Trim the smaller pom-pom to form a neat round shape for the Bird's head. Trim the larger pom-pom to create the shape for the body, leaving the wool longer around the Bird's bottom to look like tail feathers. ✹

TIP! *Pom-poms are all about the trimming. Don't be worried that you're trimming a lot of excess wool.*

7. Using a large needle threaded with wool 8 in/20 cm long, thread the needle through the bottom of the body and up through the head. Loop the wool back through the top of the head and through the body, then tie in a knot at the bottom to hold them together. You can also dab glue between the head and the body to make it extra secure before sewing. ✹

8. Photocopy the templates from page 46. Using the photocopy as a guide, cut the Bird's wings out of green felt. Apply glue to the straight edges of the felt wings and tuck them into the sides of the Bird's body.

9. Using the template on page 46, cut the beak out of orange felt, apply glue to the end and tuck it in place at the front of the Bird's head. Glue the plastic eyes in position on either side of the Bird's head. ✹

10. Tie the ribbon around the Bird's neck. Your Bird should look like the photo on page 33.

3.

6.

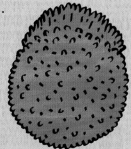

7.

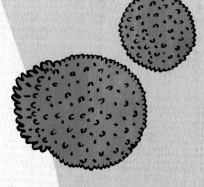

9.

VARIATION

For a spring chick, use yellow wool, dark orange for the beak, lighter orange felt for the wings, and a red ribbon.

GIANT POM

OWL

No one can resist a sweet owl, especially a quirky multicolored one. You can choose whatever colors you like for the wool, as long as it is really thick and textured. When trimming the pom-pom, leave it rough around the edges to look like feathers.

materials you'll need

Extra-thick multicolored wool (approx 2 ¼ oz/60 g; binding: approx 12 in/30 cm)

Templates from page 47

Pink felt

White felt

Orange felt

Gray embroidery floss

Two plastic eyes

1. Cut a piece of thick cardboard, roughly 10¾ x 4½ in/27 cm x 12 cm.

2. Wrap the wool around the cardboard. Wrap it around with consistent and gentle tension, making sure it is not too tight, and wrap it evenly along the length of the cardboard. The wool shouldn't be fatter in the middle. Tuck the last bit of wool into the wool wrap.

3. Gently slide the bundle of wool off the cardboard, making sure you keep hold of it so that it doesn't unravel. Using a piece of wool 12 in/30 cm long, wrap the wool around the bundle horizontally, making sure it is tight. It will squeeze the wrapped wool together in the middle. ✽

4. Slide the blade of your scissors into the loops of the bundle and gradually work your way around, until you have a rough pom-pom. Shape it into an oval. ✽

5. Photocopy the templates from page 47. Using the templates as a guide, cut out the outer circles for the eyes in pink felt and the inner circles in white felt. Glue them together and leave to dry. Use a straight stitch and gray embroidery floss to sew around the white part of the Owl's eye onto the pink part. Cut a little hole in the middle of the eye and insert the black plastic eye. ✽

TIP! You can also add a dab of glue to the plastic eye to secure it in place.

6. Using the templates on page 47 as a guide, cut out the Owl's beak from the orange felt and the Owl's wings from the pink felt. ✽

7. Apply glue to the straight edges of the wings and attach them to either side of the pom-pom. Glue the beak and eyes to the front of the pom-pom to create a face. Leave to dry. Your Owl should look like the photo on page 36.

3.

4.

5.

6.

VARIATION

Add two feet to the bottom of the Owl. Cut a semicircle from yellow felt, then shape the flat edge of the semicircle with a few snips of the scissors to form a zigzag that looks like three toes. Repeat for the other foot. Glue underneath the pom-pom and leave to dry.

PUPPY

Puppy has adorable droopy ears and a cute collar that can be adapted to any color ribbon or shape of bead that you wish. Any dog lover will find him hard to resist.

. . . .

1. Cut a piece of thick cardboard, roughly 4½ in x 2¾ in/12 cm x 7 cm.

2. Wrap the black wool around the cardboard. Wrap it around with consistent and gentle tension, making sure it is not too tight, and wrap it evenly along the length of the cardboard. The wool shouldn't be fatter in the middle. Tuck the last bit of wool into the wool wrap.

3. Gently slide the bundle of wool off the cardboard, making sure you keep hold of it so that it doesn't unravel. Using a piece of wool 12 in/30 cm long, wrap the wool around the bundle horizontally, making sure it is tight. It will squeeze the wrapped wool together in the middle.

4. Slide the blade of your scissors into the loops of the bundle and gradually work your way around, until you have a rough pom-pom.

materials you'll need

Thick black wool
(body: approx 1 ¼ oz/35 g;
head: approx 1 oz/25 g;
binding for head and body:
32 in/80 cm)

Templates from page 47

Black felt

White felt

Black embroidery floss

Two plastic eyes

One plastic nose

Yellow ribbon

Red star button

PEDIGREE POM

5. Repeat steps 1 to 4 for the Puppy's head, using less wool to create a slightly smaller pom-pom.

6. Trim the smaller pom-pom to form a neat round shape for the Puppy's head. Trim the larger pom-pom to create the Puppy's body so that it has a flat top and body and straighter sides. ✸

7. Using a large needle threaded with wool 8 in/20 cm long, thread the needle through the bottom of the body and up through the head. Loop the wool back through the top of the head and through the body, then tie in a knot at the bottom to hold them together. You can also dab glue between the head and the body to make it extra secure before stitching.

8. Photocopy the templates on page 47. Using the template as a guide, cut out the Puppy's ears from black felt.

9. Pinch the flat edge of each ear to form a pleat and, using a needle and black floss, stitch in place. ✸

10. Apply glue to the pinched edge of each ears and wedge the ears into the sides of the pom-pom head so that they droop downward. ✸

11. Using the templates on page 47 cut out the Puppy's nose from brown felt. Cut a small hole in the nose and insert the black plastic nose. Add a black vertical stitch to the felt below the nose.

TIP! Use pins to keep the photocopy in place on top of the felt and cut around the lines of the template through the two layers.

12. Glue the black plastic eyes and nose to the Puppy's head. Leave to dry. ✸

13. Using the template on page 47 as a guide, cut the Puppy's feet out of the black felt. Wedge the paws near the base of the body pom-pom so that they droop down a little, rather than gluing them to the bottom of the pom-pom.

14. Finally, glue or sew the red star button in place on the ribbon, wrap the ribbon around the Puppy's neck and glue or stitch it at the back.

4.

6.

9.

10.

12.

VARIATION

Make the Puppy's body from two different shades of wool. Draw a line halfway down the cardboard to act as a guide. Wrap half the cardboard with white wool and the other half with black wool. Trim the pom-pom so the white part is smaller than the black, to give him a white belly.

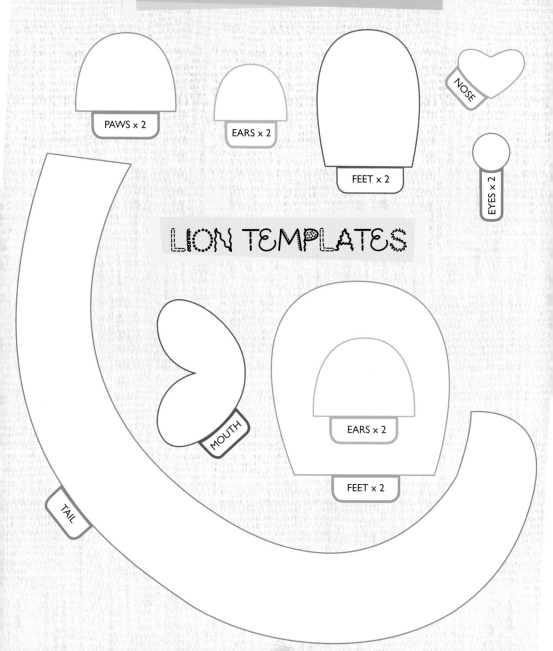

HEDGEHOG TEMPLATES

PAWS x 2

EARS x 2

FEET x 2

NOSE

EYES x 2

LION TEMPLATES

MOUTH

EARS x 2

FEET x 2

TAIL

44

RABBIT TEMPLATES

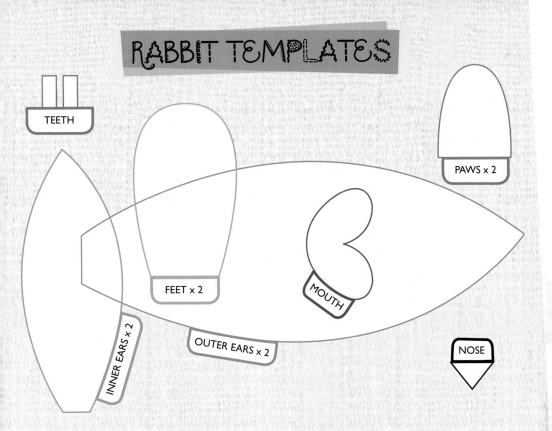

TEETH

PAWS x 2

FEET x 2

MOUTH

INNER EARS x 2

OUTER EARS x 2

NOSE

TEDDY TEMPLATES

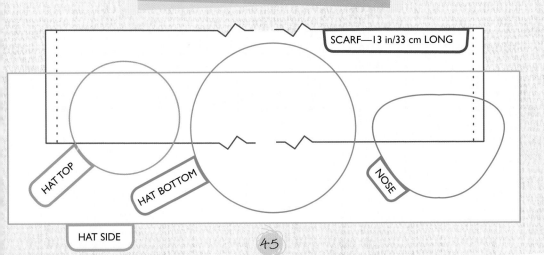

SCARF—13 in/33 cm LONG

HAT TOP

HAT BOTTOM

NOSE

HAT SIDE

CAT TEMPLATES

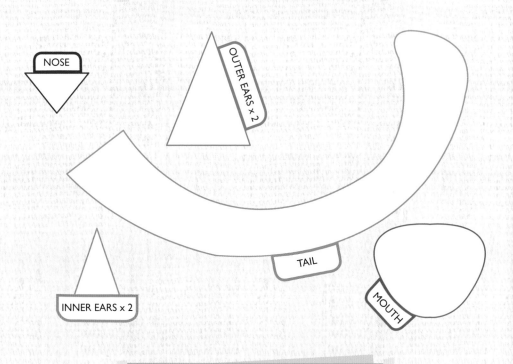

NOSE

OUTER EARS x 2

TAIL

MOUTH

INNER EARS x 2

BIRD TEMPLATES

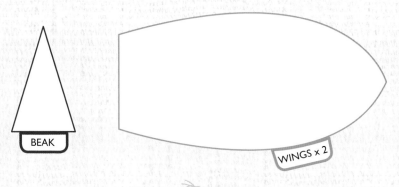

BEAK

WINGS x 2

46

OWL TEMPLATES

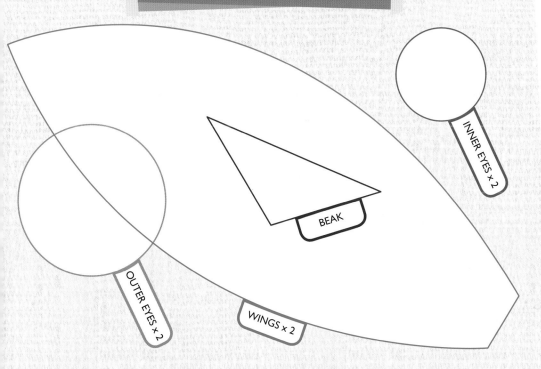

INNER EYES × 2

BEAK

OUTER EYES × 2

WINGS × 2

PUPPY TEMPLATES

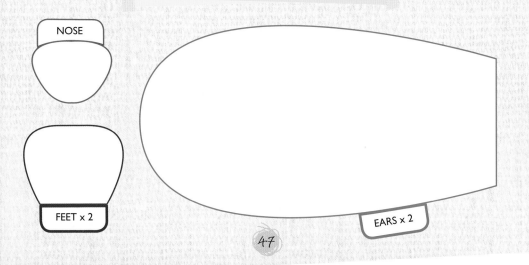

NOSE

FEET × 2

EARS × 2

47